SCARED TO BE ME

Nathan A. Webster

AuthorHouse™
1663 Liberty Drive
Bloomington, IN 47403
www.authorhouse.com
Phone: 1 (800) 839-8640

Dream Big Community Center
PO Box 871921
Vancouver, WA 98687
(360) 448-7439

Editing Contributions: Sarah Chivers
Rebekah Dull

All graphic design by Lavell Alexander, Elan Motif Designs.

Published by AuthorHouse: 09/03/2015

ISBN: 978-1-5049-2633-1 (sc)
ISBN: 978-1-5049-2634-8 (e)

Print information available on the last page.

Any people depicted in stock imagery provided by Thinkstock are models,
and such images are being used for illustrative purposes only.
Certain stock imagery © Thinkstock.

This book is printed on acid-free paper.

authorHOUSE®

SCARED TO BE ME

Nathan A. Webster, MBA

FOREWORD

If it wasn't for God waking me up one night and giving me this idea, I would not be writing this to you. This book is dedicated to my kiddos that are my mini me's. I love them, and I don't want them to ever make the same mistakes I did.

This book is for anyone. We all have dreams. The question is, are you scared to pursue it? It took me awhile to answer that question. And obviously, I answered it after a long battle with myself.

Your battle with yourself will be victorious if you take it one day at a time. Don't worry about others. Just do you. And you'll be fine!

Enjoy the read.

TABLE OF CONTENTS

MY FEAR

When I was a young boy, around the 5th grade, I wanted to be someone else. I didn't want to be the person I saw in the mirror. I saw ugliness. It wasn't me, at least not what I wanted to see.

I wanted to be good looking. I wanted to be strong. I wanted to feel wanted.

I wanted to be fast. I wanted to be popular. I wanted to be liked.

The person in the mirror that I saw wasn't who I wanted to be.

Deep down inside, **I was lost**. I was searching and looking for someone to relate to… Why didn't everyone look like me?

In frustrating thoughts, I would ask…

Does anyone see me?
Can someone please see me?
Was I too fat?
Do I talk funny?
Was I too short?
Did I smell?
Do I dress funny?
Was I too black?
Was I too tall?
What's wrong with me?
Am I the only one who stands out?
Am I alone?

I wanted to be accepted for who I was. I wanted to have friends. I wanted them to want me as a friend. I wanted to believe in others, and I wanted them to believe in me.

I wanted us to have the same likes and dislikes. I wanted my friends to always be my friends. I didn't want us to have fights. We would get along with everyone, and never make enemies.

Really, I just wanted to be happy. That's all. I wondered if being happy would ever happen to me. I just wanted to be accepted, and have a friend.

When I was growing up, I wasn't happy. Unfortunately, I was scared to accept who I was, what I looked like, and who I could be. **I was afraid** to be the boy I saw in the mirror. Matter of fact, I was scared to look at him most of the time. Honestly, I would reject what I saw. I was scared to look at me.

As I grew older, that fear never left. The boy in the mirror was still scared at the age of 18, even in my 20's. I was scared to be me. I wanted to be anyone else but me.

In my late 20's, life would make sense all of a sudden. Throughout my adulthood while making many mistakes, I began to find that guy in the mirror wasn't so bad. He was good looking, kind, funny, and smart. Before I knew it, I couldn't stop looking in the mirror. And then finally it happened, I started to fall in love with that scared little boy in the mirror.

I took a long and windy road to love me. Loving me was hard, but not impossible. I had lots to love about myself, but I didn't know how nor was I shown how to love me.

Once I started to love me, so many things became easy. I began to have the courage I've always lacked. I was no longer scared of looking myself in the mirror when I discovered what made me happy. Those things were my funny sense of humor, my big smile, my love for sports, my obnoxious laugh, the ability to solve complex problems and to create unique things. When I looked in the mirror, I would almost act as if I had a cape on because I stood tall and proud.

I eventually learned that the mirror shouldn't be an enemy. I had to embrace the mirror, reaffirming all the good. I would say all the things my counselor told me that I thought was silly. You ARE *smart, intelligent, cool, witty, fun, innovative,* and *comical.* At first, it was weird and awkward. After a while, I was like- of course I am, silly!

When you find something that you can do, it will keep you up at night. **I mean *really, really* do well**, you won't stop. All the things you thought you liked to do will soon fade away to be side activities. All of those things you doubted you could be, you'll find yourself being them. And I'm not talking about after you accomplish this big huge task, journey or milestone. It will be immediate.

Basically, it's as simple as finding your purpose in life. Yes, you do have a purpose.

You're really, really funny!

NATHAN W.

I'm handsome

I'm smart!

What's your sticky note?

_____

_____

_____

HAVING PURPOSE

To have purpose may sound big and extravagant, which it is, but it doesn't mean you have to climb Mount Everest to find it. And no, you don't have to be an Olympic Gold Medalist or a Super Hero to find purpose either. Purpose comes from within. Your purpose is there. If you don't know what it looks like, it's because it is in raw form.

You can find it the mirror. If you don't find it there, go for a 20 minute walk and think about what you like to do. The walk or looking in the mirror will be the starting process of finding your purpose. Don't overcomplicate it.

You may even have to **unbury** yourself from all the obstacles you placed in front of you. Some may know what stops them, some of you may not. As an adult, here are some things that stop people from having purpose:

- Money
- Degrees
- Age
- status
- geography

Talk to a couple people you know, and maybe some folks you don't know. Your purpose is not going to hit you from out of nowhere. You will have to seek it out. This will take effort.

The more I live this life, the more I realize I need purpose to ensure I'm going be happy. The purpose gives me satisfaction. The satisfaction gives self-fulfillment.

For example, when I play competitive sports with a group of people, I have to remind myself this is only for recreation. A win isn't going to impress a scout. There isn't anyone offering me a 10-day contract with a professional team. There is no sneaker or beverage deal. And I won't have a front row seat at the ESPY's. For the competitor within me, I reiterate this over and over.

Sometimes I think I'm just getting older and becoming like those guys that just watch on the sidelines, and don't want to play. But that's not it at all. I have a limited amount of time, and all of it needs to be used wisely. If I'm going to do something, I want it to have value.

To have purpose is to have meaning.

Therefore, you have a job to do. Someone needs your purpose to give them a purpose. Without you being you and contributing your special gift, everything that exists around you changes. Believe it or not, you're here to make a positive impact on our universe. It's waiting for you to make moves, talk to people, and begin living out your purpose.

Imagine if you laid around all day and never got out of bed, except to eat and use the bathroom? Stop and seriously think about that. I mean, really think about not doing anything at all.

Truly think about that!

That means you wouldn't ever leave the house and you would be closed off from the outside world. Think about your room. Your room would be different. The décor would be suited for your everyday needs. You'd have different clothes, entertainment, and social activities.

Think how many tasks would go uncompleted?

How many of your personal relationships would be different without you?

Would you have any relationships?

What about music?

Would you eat the same food?

How would your personality be different not influenced by anyone else?

Would your personality be influenced only by your parents?

More importantly, what would the world lack if you didn't make your contribution to society?

You were created to make a difference. You have value. You belong here for a reason, but it's for you to figure out what that purpose is.

To live your purpose is a gift. You're the only one that has this unique gift. No one can do… see… feel… believe… act… or be you. Everything you do is extraordinary or **EXTRA**-Ordinary!

One of my favorite quotes from Robert Schuller, "What would you do if you couldn't fail", is a powerful quote to make you think about what you're NOT doing. He makes you feel like you can do more. Achieve the impossible. Overcome all obstacles. No excuses. Right!?

"What would you do if you couldn't fail?"

Some of my biggest inspirations are from people who didn't take no for an answer. In my own interpretation of some people's accomplishments I respect, I believe they saw something no one else believed.

> *Michael Jordan didn't accept that he wasn't cut out for basketball. He demanded that the basketball world respected him as a young teen. As a basketball fan that has followed him since his first days in Chicago, it's hard to say the basketball world along with sports companies would have been so successful without his contribution (e.g. – Nike, Gatorade, Wheaties, Upper Deck, Hanes, and now his very own brand, Jordan) .*

> *Thomas Edison was not going to rest until he created a device that would illuminate a room or house upon request. He looked at every failure as a success. I believe if he didn't keep a detailed log of all his adjustments, he probably wouldn't know it took over 10,000 times to make that light bulb work.*

> *ESPN for believing that there was a demand for a sports oriented industry. I'm sure the naysayers were crowd-fulls. Being how the television was created for more serious issues, I believe a channel dedicated to only sports created quite the laughter around the executive roundtable back in the day. And now, they're owned by super juggernaut Disney and is the industry leader for sports entertainment, news, and coverage for all sports. I love my SportsCenter!*

> *My time working at Nike gave me the first true professional insight of adversity. Phil Knight (the Nike co-founder) faced extreme opposition and was even probably laughed at by Converse executives in the beginning of their inception. Who would have known 30+ years later, Nike would buy Converse and make them one of their many brands.* (Wayne)

Your purpose is only yours to have, achieve, and accomplish. No one can do what you can do. However, your purpose will take enormous self-initiative, perseverance, dedication, and courage. Ultimately, this will be an incredible investment of time. And if you're reading this book, you understand that your time is important. With the new craze of social media and 6-second videos, our attention span is shorter and more open to distractions.

Did you just want to check any of your social media sites now? LOL!

Distractions are so IN-YOUR-FACE. I can't even watch an On-Demand show without being bothered by a commercial. YouTube videos have ads. Stores have samples. Everywhere you go, you can so easily be distracted.

I'm not saying be a zombie. Distractions are not necessarily a bad thing, but they can destroy your dream and you may never find your way back onto your path of purpose if you allow them to distract you. Stay aware that everyone wants your time, but they come 2nd.

You come first.

Your purpose needs to be sought, desired, and worked on. There are no shortcuts. And everyone has their own unique way of finding theirs.

To find your purpose, you will have to find and expand your building blocks.

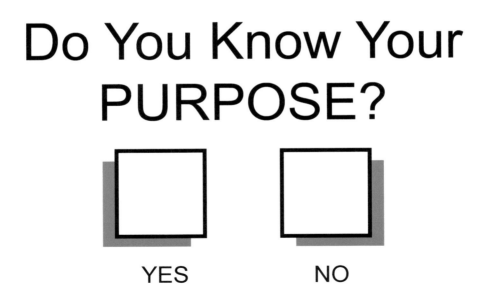

Do You Know Your PURPOSE?

YES   NO

BUILDING BLOCKS

Have you ever wanted to start something huge, but not know where to start? You say to yourself:

"Self, how am I going to do this?"

Then you have this great grandiose idea. You get really excited. The ideas are racing through your head. Ideas are coming and going so fast you can't write them down. Once you get the pencil or notes section on your electronic device, you go blank.

Or, you can't come up with anything. You spend a good amount of time thinking what to do, how to do it, or should you do it. You find yourself searching for ideas. Before you know it, you're on a totally different subject and now time has expired.

I've done both scenarios several times. No need to count, because I'm sure it would turn to into years. Just know it was a LOT.

My best recommendation **is to start small.** I'm one of those people that doesn't stop when I see what I want. I will go all night if I have to complete a project or task.

Sometimes this occurs in the last minute, and I have a rush of energy, creativity, and brainpower. I get going and I feel great about it. After a few hours, I lose steam after a while and kick myself for not starting earlier.

While I was in college, my best ideas would come to me the day or two prior to the due date. I would get so excited, because I knew this was an "A" project. I laughed because I thought I could do everything in less time than everyone else, but I would always hit a wall. Even though I would finish my project, handing it in with the utmost confidence, I would never receive the grade I thought.

Anything worth value cannot be done overnight. **Quality takes time and dedication.** Begin doing small segments. Build a foundation. Start with one, and then add another one. It's similar to learning how to walk: one foot at a time, and one in front of the other.

Your building blocks will build that foundation to stand on. To be clear and simple, you need to remove all the clutter, junk, distractions and garbage. Your beginning or start needs to be clean, strong and flat. Think of it as a lunch tray.

The lunch tray is big enough to hold (2) plates full of food, and a drink. You also put your utensils on it, such as your knife, fork, and spoon. Don't forget your napkins. And maybe, you have enough room to place your dessert on it.

Now you have everything you need to start and eat your meal without thinking you missed anything. That lunch tray was your foundation. Everything that you placed on there was a building block. In this case, your building blocks built a great meal.

When you begin to collect your building blocks, beware of cracks and chipped corners. The blocks must be of quality. Don't go cheap, nor rush it or be in a hurry. They need to be sturdy and useful. Inspect all of them, because they cannot be damaged or weak.

For example, if I wanted to become a dessert chef—which is also known as a pastry chef—to be the best chocolate chip cookie maker in the world, I would need to start somewhere. **Again, don't overthink it**. Start simple by collecting recipes from a cookbook. I would have to obtain some baking necessities: mixing bowl, spatula, whisk, cookie sheet, and cooling racks.

I would also need to have the right ingredients. Can't forget the basics of a working oven and timer. Recruit people to become my tasters. In 10 to 15 minutes later of placing the cookie dough in the oven, I would have begun my very first attempts of making my dream come true.

Imagine yelling with an echo in the background, "*I'M GOING TO BAKE THE BEST CHOCOLATE CHIP COOKIES IN THE WORLD!*"

Again… That's if my dream was to be a dessert chef. Everyone likes sweets.

Is that your dream?

Do you have any ideas of what you want to do?

The building blocks are your starting point. Building blocks come in many forms, so don't be picky. If you don't know where to start to find building blocks, start with anything you have direct access to or a basic understanding. Here are some immediate resources at your fingertips, such as:

- Books
- Advice
- Equipment
- Magazines
- Documentaries
- Professionals
- Experience
- Manuals
- Ideas

And if you **STILL** *don't know where to go, who to ask, start at the Bureau of Labor and Statistics website, and go to their Occupational Page. Here's the link: www.bls.gov/ooh.*

They will set you up for success, but the **building blocks alone will not give you success**. To find success, you will have to try and find what works for you.

This process is called, Trial and Failure.

TRIAL & FAILURE

I'm sure you have heard the saying, "just be you." If not, let me introduce you to it. That saying was hard for me, because I never knew who I was. I never tried to find me, so I wouldn't know how to be.

In the 5th grade, my teacher assigned us to do an autobiography, AND we had to take a picture. This was back in the day when you only took an individual picture once a year, your school picture.

There were no cell phones. We still used corded phones that were hung up on the walls. I always had a $0.25 in my bag for payphones.

For my picture, I made sure I did my hair to look like everyone else. It wasn't my first choice. **My plan A failed**. Plan A started when I relaxed my hair with a very popular product that straightened my hair, which was opposite of what I wanted. It was supposed to make it really wavy, but it didn't. Since I couldn't get my waves right (what black men's hair will do when the curls lie flat), I went to plan B.

I improvised and made it into the cool hairstyle of all my buddies. At the time, it was a successful accomplishment for me. But when I look back on it, I wanted to be something I could never be. I wanted to be white for so many reasons, which would fix the issues I thought I had. This was a deeper and larger issue with myself at that time, and I was completely lost of what skin color meant. Fortunately, this period of confusion was only temporary.

My attempt to be white was **never successful**. I eventually accepted that I was black, and nothing was going to change that. I had to accept it. It was hard at first, but it became easier the more I accepted it. I'm proud of my ethnic background, African-American. I'm proud to be black.

You see, I saw my skin color and not my rich history of being from Africa. Even though I have other ethnicities within me, I began to embrace who I saw in the mirror. I finally accepted what was in the mirror, and I was okay with that.

* Now that you know mine, what's your struggle? Everybody's struggle is different. Don't be afraid, because you're not alone.

My trial and failure to be another ethnicity allowed me to conquer the **hateful things** I believed about myself. When I believed the names I was called, that meant everything that included being those names. Those hurtful names I shall not repeat, but these are the feelings they left me with:

- Worthless
- Dumb
- Ugly
- Stupid
- Different

- Ashamed
- Alien
- Outcast
- Replaceable
- Rejected

None of those names were true, and they don't matter. But words still hurt. They cannot be retracted.

Those names still come to haunt me today when I want to accomplish a cool idea. However, I learned that I cannot be scared to try because of what someone told me 20 to 30 years ago. I have to ignore "that kid" inside of me who is scared and hides under the bed when those feelings emerge.

He's never really that far from me, but he will quietly appear and begins to whisper those hurtful names to me as if it was my first time hearing those names.

"Nathan, you can't do that because you're _____!"

As he whispers those cruel words, those feelings inflict the pain and take me back to my past. Then he starts to play peek-a-boo with me. His playfulness distracts me from staying on task.

There's no way for me to ignore him. I can't deny it never happened. It's my past, but it isn't my present. I deny the game he wants to play, but I do acknowledge he's there and inform him we're not playing that game. And he goes away.

I accepted starting anything new is scary. Anything new will create those nerves and butterflies in your stomach. It's okay to try and fail, but it's not okay to not try because you believe the lies of others telling you it won't work.

Don't give in or give up because someone is saying it won't work. Expect those comments to be said so you won't be surprised. In any circumstance, you telling yourself it won't work is unacceptable and wrong.

When you don't do what you believe in, figure out why. For me, I didn't want to believe I was smart or good enough. For you, there's a reason. Whatever that reason is, don't be scared to take the time and learn why you're playing peek-a-boo with those that don't like or believe in you.

And… Usually, the TRY isn't really the hard piece. No one wants to TRY and be REJECTED. It's hard to be rejected, but it's not always a bad thing.

Rejection has a **bad reputation**. This is unfortunate.

One may ask, why?

The logic or reasoning behind rejection is that you're a failure, and that couldn't be more false then saying that you talk with your ears. FALSE! You're not a failure. If you are not successful at your first or second or third attempt, that means you need more time and more attempts.

The FAILURE is the hardest part to understand. Not everyone deals with failure the same. We all have our own way to process the feelings of failure or rejection. For some, this means to quit. For others, it means to try a different way.

There have been many great successful athletes, musicians, entrepreneurs, actors, educators, professionals, and many more that have been laughed at. Many have faced gargantuan giants, sharp spears to their ideas, and rapid fiery denials. I personally like Nike's Co-Founder and Chairman, Phil Knight's history , and FedEx Founder, CEO (Chief Executive Officer) and Chairman, Frederick Smith's story. Those gentlemen are highly regarded entrepreneurs, millionaires, and successful professionals in their industry.

* If you want to learn their background, you have to read their story on your own. Both were educated and denied to pursue their dream. It'll help you with finding your purpose. Wink!

I'm nowhere close to making comparisons to my dream similar to those superstar individuals, but both of them found what they wanted to do in a higher learning environment. **That's where I found my dream.** I was in the last place I ever wanted to be when I was a kid, teenager, and even a high school graduate. I was in college.

My fear of going to college was strong. I was never told I needed to go to college by my parents, but they never told me not to go either. When colleges reached out to me, I never responded because I believed I wasn't smart enough. Matter of fact, I laughed at letters they sent. Later on in life, I came to the conclusion that I needed college.

If I never went to college, **I would have never found myself.** That means my passion would still be floating out there in the universe for me to pursue. Funny, the place I never wanted to go, transformed into my favorite playground where I could explore and create. Yay, college!

How would I know college was going to be fun? I was scared. I didn't want to fail. As a child, I didn't believe I was smart. Therefore, I didn't try to go to college after high school. I ran the opposite direction into the United States Marine Corps.

Again, this was me not embracing myself as who I was.

For some reason, we as a society hate to say fail or failure. It's not like a dark cloud will immediately start pouring rain over your head. Lol! The key is to learn from the failed attempts, and apply your learnings to make the next one better.

Failure is inevitable and necessary to make anything successful. Failure is an event, not a characteristic.

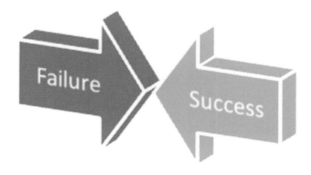

SUCCESS

Okay, we've talked about failure. Now it's time to talk about success. I believe this is one of many words that create more definitions than any other word. Please pay attention very carefully.

If you need to re-read this, please do so.

I wanted to show you a screenshot of what the definition of success means.

WAIT! STOP!

Don't look at the definitions just yet. These words are all nouns except the word succeed. What's a noun? Traditionally, we know a noun to be a person, place or thing. Meaning, these are all currently in existence. So now apply this to your idea.

Doesn't that mean it already exists? YES, you are correct!

Now look at the definitions. Do you see that all the definitions have **sublinks** to other words?

You see, success is a living and evolving word (Merriam-Webster, Incorporated).

As you see in all the screenshots, the definitions of the others, such as: outcome, succeed, and eminence all have constant definitions (Merriam-Webster, Incorporated).

Take a couple of minutes and read the definitions.

Do you see the word success can never be constant?

Success is a nurturer. Within the definition, the word continues to provide nutrients to those building blocks, and creates a consistent glue-like bond that can never be broken. Your success is a living nutrient and will be self-staining as long you believe in purpose, and stay persistent.

Full Definition of SUCCESS
1obsolete : OUTCOME, RESULT
2a : degree or measure of succeeding
b : favorable or desired outcome; also : the attainment of wealth, favor, oreminence
3: one that succeeds

Full Definition of **EMINENCE**
1: a position of prominence or superiority
2: one that is eminent, prominent, or lofty: as
a : an anatomical protuberance (as on a bone)
b : a person of high rank or attainments —often used as a title for a cardinal
c : a natural elevation

Full Definition of **SUCCEED**
intransitive verb
1a: to come next after another in office or position or in possession of an estate; *especially*: to inherit sovereignty, rank, or title
b: to follow after another in order
2a: to turn out well
b: to attain a desired object or end <students who *succeed* in college>
3obsolete: to pass to a person by inheritance
transitive verb
1: to follow in sequence and especially immediately
2: to come after as heir or successor

Full Definition of OUTCOME
: something that follows as a result or consequence

Let me show you:

Basic Concept

Attempt → Fail → Another Attempt→ Success

Basic Idea Process

Idea #1 → Fail → Fix the issue → Success

The basic concept diagram shows how to accomplish something new to them, but not new to existence. For example, let's start with creating a new email. When you create an email password for new account, you'll have another chance if you complete it incorrectly. If you don't have the correct characters, you will need to try again. Once it's completed correctly, you'll successfully created your new account. However, an email account isn't a new concept. But let's keep it to those yummy cookies so it doesn't get too confusing.

The basic idea diagram shows how to bring a new concept to reality. This simple diagram lacks the number of failure, time it takes, and how many solutions it took to solve the issue. This was to show the basic framework of trial and failure. Continue with me to the concept and baking cookies.

The basic baking chocolate cookie process diagram shows all the stages from ingredients to eating them. At any given time, any of the processes can be done incorrectly and have your eating experience differ each time. This is where trial and failure comes in. Until those processes can be done successfully each time, your world's best ever chocolate cookie will always be inconsistent.

Basic Baking Chocolate Cookie Process

Prep → Mix → Stir → Ball → Bake → Time → Cool → Eat

We buy cookies in packages because we want all of them to taste the same. In order for them to taste the same, they all need to be consistent. Meaning, each cookie has gone through the same processes. All those **processes are your building blocks**. Each building block will be a learned success, which means your cookie baking process will soon be free from errors once you find which method works best.

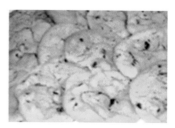

Once you develop that "know how" to ensure every process is successful, you continue to build upon that foundation. Those building blocks are now the things that become who you are. In most cases, it has now become tangible. Meaning, you have some type of proof that your idea works how you envisioned.

Inventors and business people would call this a proof of concept.

Now that you have proof of a good cookie, great reviews, and a verified process that works, that doesn't mean you have success. You have just begun.

Many believe that success is the end, or a destination. Here's the mistake many will make:

"I'm ready to take it to bakeries and start selling. But no one wants to buy my cookies."

or

"I still have way too much to do. This is never going to end."

The execution may not be perfected, but that's okay. No one may want to buy right now, that's okay. They may not be packaged with commercial wrapping, and that's okay too. Take the time to celebrate your success. Remember, **you just begun.** You still have a lot of work to do.

This is why "Trial and Failure" is necessary.

The beautiful thing about your success is that you have already seen it. You know what it is. You know what it looks like. It's your vision. Remember, success is a noun. A noun is a person, place or thing. In this case, make it applicable to your dream:

Person: You or you know who else you want to be involved.

Place: You know where this immediately needs to be.

Thing: You have envisioned what it looks like in your imagination.

For your idea to succeed, the steps to build your success will be ongoing. To have your dream/purpose succeed means you took what you envisioned, and made it your reality. To be successful, is what you have imagined what's going to happen and the realities are blended together.

The only thing you can't predict is time. Quality will take time.

Again, nothing of great quality can be done overnight.

download your thoughts

TIME

The basic but underestimated component of accomplishing something would be time. Time never stops. It is constant- although sometimes time might not feel constant (that hour in economics class feels longer than that hour on the basketball court or video game), we do track time down to the second.

Here are some cool examples of time:

In Physics: Gravity falls at – 9.8 m/s^2 (meter per second)

In Humans: The Olympic World Record for the 100 meter dash – 9.58 seconds (Burfoot).

In Cars: Fastest car from 0 to 60mph (miles per hour) –Maxximus G-Force accomplished that in 2.1 seconds (Motor Trend).

In Animals: Cheetah – 71mph (miles per hour) (The Travel Almanac)

In Fish: Sailfish – 68mph (miles per hour) (The Travel Almanac)

In Birds: Peregrine Falcon – more than 200mph (miles per hour) (The Travel Almanac)

Have you noticed the majority of our records are for the fastest or the shortest amount of time? For some reason, we like fast things. A fast pitched baseball, fast forward through video or skip functions when we listen to music, fast food to go when in a hurry, and overnight delivery (especially during the holidays). Not only do we like it fast, we want it now. It's called **instant gratification**.

As a kid, one of the things I wanted immediately was to be skinny. I wasn't obese, but I had some extra layers to keep me warm during the cold weather. It was enough layers that my peers called me names. I was called all kind of fat names. They would make fat jokes to me, and even tell them in front of me. They thought they were funny. I did not.

I laughed with them but I never considered them my friends. I was scared to stand up for myself. I didn't know how to embrace different personalities, bodies, and appearances. All I knew is that I was different, and I didn't like it.

The dream I wanted was to be skinny and fast (like a fast runner). Those were the guys that got all the attention, popular and received special treatment. They even hung around the pretty girls. I knew if I could lose all the weight and be really fast, I could have all of that.

Well, in the 9th grade while I was in junior high, I finally got my first girlfriend. Our relationship lasted for about two weeks, and I began losing a considerable amount of weight. From playing football, not eating that much, talking on the phone with her every night, I had lost approximately 60 pounds in 3 months. It wasn't instantaneous, but I also wasn't trying. I dropped down from 275 to 215.

I remember one of my coaches challenged me to get down to 190 for the wrestling weight class, and I thought I could. I lost so much weight from the beginning of the school year, my body hit a plateau. Meaning, I wasn't ready to break that milestone yet. When I couldn't reach the goal that my coach had challenged me to, I felt like a failure and he didn't appreciate my accomplishment. Again, nothing I did was ever good enough.

Unbeknown to me, my life would be forever changed from those three months. Those three months in comparison to my entire high school career, military career, and entire life, it is equal to a speck of dust on a table. That time flew by extremely fast.

When looking back, all I needed were two weeks to change my bad habits; but to also realize that I could lose weight. The following year, I wrestled at 190 and voted by the coaches as **Most Improved** at the end of the season. Not only did I reach my goal, but my accomplishment was acknowledged by everyday efforts of doing my best.

Even though I wanted to be skinnier a few years earlier, I was very happy I finally lost the weight. The timing was not perfect, but nothing is perfect. To have the right timing takes patience and commitment. If you want time to work for you, first understand how time works.

First of all, time is constant. It never changes. Time doesn't stop.

Secondly, you need to know how to apply your goals with correct measurements.

Thirdly, realize that nothing is perfect.

Lastly, to plan out the **RIGHT** timing of the right steps and in the right order would be impossible. Again, remember nothing is perfect. Here are five tips to handle an issue or idea:

1. Have a plan
2. Place a timeline on your plan
3. Work your plan
4. Don't quit on your plan
5. Evaluate and revise your plan

For example, our pastry chef baking chocolate chip cookies may possibly want a bakery to sell to customers and businesses. A simple timeline would look like:

3 to 6 months:	*Obtain business license*
6 to 12 months:	*Certify personal kitchen with health inspectors*
1st to 2nd year:	*Acquire several returning customers*
2nd to 5th year:	*Open bakery*

As we operate in a world of fast, express, and overnight, be careful not to rush the things you want. Anything worth value comes with the price of time. Don't expect what you want to come instantaneously.

I knew… seriously, **I KNEW I could defy** the odds of time, but I quickly learned fast isn't always good.

One of my college professors told me, "Don't be like me, a victim of my own success." I didn't understand, so I asked for clarification. She explained how she focused more on achieving the degree than her career. That still took me some time to process, but I finally understood. As for my understanding, I applied it carefully to not overlook anything or get caught up in the hype.

Don't get me wrong, my competitive nature loves to finish first. I'm sure you do too. However, it isn't about placing or standing on a podium. This is about ensuring your dream can be done for the rest of your life.

Timing does matter. Timing will matter a great deal to ensure your accomplish your dream. However, you may also need to make some sacrifices.

What GOALS do you want to accomplish in the following:

6 Months

1st Year

3rd Year

5th Year

SACRIFICE

This is a word that is very rarely discussed. I don't ever remember hearing about sacrifices when I grew up. Matter of fact, I don't think anyone told me to make a sacrifice or sacrifices were needed to be made in order to achieve my purpose.

The Merriam-Webster Dictionary captures it best, "the act of giving up something that you want to keep especially in order to get something else" (Merriam-Webster, Incorporated). In other words, you have to give to receive. When you give something to sacrifice, it is from the heart. And no, we're not talking about an item you're thinking about donating or giving away. **A true sacrifice** is close to the heart, which means you don't want to give it up. Therefore, it's called a sacrifice.

We as human beings hate giving up our prized and precious possessions. The items we have collected, earned, or have been given are special. And those things can be anything from time, money, automobiles, electronics, jewelry, food, looks, entertainment, or status. Hopefully, you understand that it truly can be anything. Nothing is excluded.

For example, in order for our pastry chef to meet their timetable, they would have to sacrifice their personal space and appliances. In a residential kitchen, this process is hard but not impossible. To make room for commercial equipment and an area suited to meet health and safety standards is a big deal.

If you have a family, there would have to be designated time and areas specifically for the business. The dry and cool storage would be very minimal for personal snacks, vegetables, favorite meals, or special desserts. The kitchen can no longer be a hangout spot. These adjustments would be sacrifices.

Full Definition of **SACRIFICE**

: the act of giving up something that you want to keep especially in order to get or do something else or to help someone

: an act of killing a person or animal in a religious ceremony as an offering to please a god

: a person or animal that is killed in a sacrifice

1: an act of offering to a deity something precious; *especially* : the killing of a victim on an altar

2: something offered in sacrifice

3a: destruction or surrender of something for the sake of something else

b: something given up or lost <the *sacrifices* made by parents>

4: LOSS <GOODS SOLD AT A *SACRIFICE*>

5: SACRIFICE HIT

The kitchen as we know where families spend a lot of time doing different bonding activities, would now change. Our pastry chef-in-the-making is taking away valuable and never to get back memories. In the long run, the chef is creating the expectation of sacrificing now and gain will come later.

The hope for the chef and family is that all the sacrifices will be worth it. After they open up the full-scale bakery and be known for the best chocolate chip cookie in the world, the sacrifices would have been worth it. As the saying goes, *"Work hard now, play hard later."*

If this was me we were talking about when I was little, I was scared to give up anything that made me happy. My major sacrifice would have been to deny the personal pleasure of unhealthy food (sweets & fast food), inactive habits (not exercising & watching television), and lying (bad character building). All these things were connected and unhealthy for me.

One may have ask, *"Why wouldn't I stop the bad habits to have a good one?"* At the time, I didn't know. I didn't care, so it didn't matter.

To sacrifice, calls for courage. The **bravery** it takes to make personal sacrifices is not for a person who prefers instant gratification. However, it has to be an individual who is willing and ready to accept responsibility for the actions needed to accomplish the goal(s), and will be willing to do what is necessary.

Remember, a sacrifice is to give. To truly give, means there are no regrets or any expectation of a reward for that act.

Your reward will be in your purpose. Your reward will come in the timing needed to extend and increase your building blocks. The sacrifice will be the increase you need to solidify your foundation.

When I was nine years old, my mom and I went to the Coney Island arcade (in New York) and played a coin game. Nowadays, this game is known as the Coin Dozer. The arcade Coin Dozer used actual quarters on the surface. We continued to feed this machine quarters to win a prize thinking we almost could tip out all the quarters and win a huge cash prize to show everyone. After hours of playing, we won a whole bunch of tickets.

This **was a complete disappointment** to us.

In foolishness, we sacrificed something good (a ride) for a horrible consequence (walking). We foolishly spent our money for bus fare on the coin dozer game, so we had to walk a very long boardwalk to get home in 100 degree scorching weather. The walk was long and hot.

We didn't have any money to buy food or drink. On the way home, we vowed to never play a money game like that again. My mom and I laughed about it years later, but we weren't laughing back then.

Life will always present us with sacrifices. Sacrifices have negative and positive consequences. We may not know we're making a sacrifice, so it's important to speak with someone when you're making this type of decision.

As the saying goes, "if it's too good to be true, well… it is." Sacrifices are non-refundable, so make sure you receive counsel before the act is done.

The counsel you'll need will come from your supporting cast.

SUPPORTING CAST

All my life, I have been very fortunate to have been blessed with a loving family and good people around me at all times. My biggest supporter would be my mother. She has always sacrificed and gave me what she could. She's been my soccer coach during the elementary and junior high years, my cheerleader during my football games—yes, she's was with the cheerleaders during my games—in high school years, and was always available to me when I was lonely at night and needed someone to call. The Marine Corps years were hard when I was thousands of miles away from my loved ones.

One of my favorite memories is when I went to visit her when I was going to school during the day and working graveyard. We lived in the same apartment complex. I was actually done with my classes for the day. When I walked in, she asked me if I was hungry. I was really just stopping by to say hi. She was relaxed and watching television. I was honest, and told her yes. Without hesitation, she popped up and asked if she could make me one of my favorite foods, French toast. "Of course I want some. But you know you don't have to do that, mom. " And then she would do her regular, "ahhhh baby, it's nothing- I don't mind."

Even though, my mom has been my biggest supporter in my supporting cast, she's let me down a few times when I really needed her. She's made plenty of mistakes but I'm not mad at her. Matter of fact, **I confronted her** with all of them and she has apologized. I wasn't a perfect child, so I'm not pointing the finger. She has always been genuine and supported me in my time of need.

My mom has always been the leader in my supporting cast. How about you? Do you have someone's name to put in these following questions? Take a minute and see if you have anyone or multiple people to list.

Here are the questions:

Do you have someone that is genuinely there with you during your struggles? _____

Do you have anyone that you trust with secrets? _____

Can you talk to more than one person about personal issues? Who? _____

Is there anyone that truly cares about you? _____

Are any of these people you sought out in your building blocks? _____

Did you ever have anyone to support you throughout your entire life? _____

I know that I've started this with a direct family member using my mom, but I also have a direct family member that never decided to have a relationship with me, my father. I believe he tried. I do believe he loved me, but he never got past the parent role to have a personal relationship. I'm not mad at him. I truly believe he did the best he knew how. Unfortunately, his best wasn't what was best for me.

My parents divorced when I was 16. However, it was always an unpleasant marriage from my perspective. I had a great family from the outside, but it was horrible within. I'm glad that I was the youngest of two from my mom and four from my dad, because I was making too many bad decisions and needed help (*I don't know what it would be like if I had younger siblings*). Little did I know, I had a whole army of people looking out for me.

For a middle-class family living in the suburbs, no kid should be making bad decisions but there I was. I was looking for all types of mischief and couldn't find it. When I was happy to find it, I had people saying things to me I didn't want to hear.

"Nathan, what you doing here?"

"Get out of here, man. You don't want to get caught up in this."

"What? You want in on this? Nah man."

"If your parents caught me doing this, you know how much trouble I'd get into? No, I'm cool. You ain't about to get me in trouble."

"You're too good for this."

At the time, none of those things mattered to me. I wanted in. I wanted to be part of the crowd. I knew I wasn't supposed to be doing any of it, but I didn't know what else to do. Remember, I was scared to be me. I didn't know how to fit in. Fortunately for me, I had people around me that cared about my well-being. They were a support system and I didn't even know it.

Those people were placed there from the beginning. My parents were hard workers, faithful church goers, and one of them was always involved with us kids in some way. Even the extracurricular activities I chose had really good people always watching out for me. They all had great character, integrity and morals. And last but not least, my friends all came from the same background. We had good homes along with moral-building activities.

As I've gotten older, those good people were harder to find. It became tougher to find people that shared the same views and lifestyles. I learned my choices stemmed for different reasons, and didn't need explanation. Those friends I considered to be my supporting cast, we're not supporting me at all. They were all just people that I knew.

One of the best things my father taught me, "You will only have one or two best friends, a few friends, and all the rest will be associates." I quickly learned there will be several people disguised as "my friends." A true friend would have my back and care about me. Those "friends" I thought I had were not there for me. They used me, made fun of me, and stole from me.

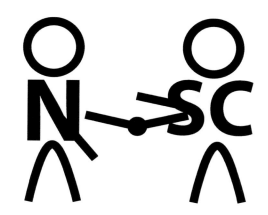

My supporting cast needed to be people who truly loved me for me. I didn't have to lie or be different for them to accept me. They listened to all that I said. They believed in me. I was considered an asset, and they were happy to have me in their life and vice versa.

Being scared to be me was **affecting the very people** I needed in my life. I choose some pretty bad people to share a life with. They were an emotional vacuum. All they did was take, and were a negative influence on my dreams.

For years, those people devalued my background, family, values, and dreams. Once I stopped being scared to be me, I realized that all those peoples were haters and nay-sayers. That's all they knew, and I needed to kick them to the curb and not look back.

Any notes?

Tinny thoughts?

Observations?

HATERS OR NAY SAYERS

When you were young, did you ever say I'm going to be a hater during career day? Lol!

I never recall learning in pre-school or kindergarten that is ok to be mean or negative. Back in my day, it wasn't normal to have haters or naysayers in your life. I remember we were all supposed to get along and become friends. Everyone was to share, be kind to others, and have fun with one another. Of course, the keyword is *supposed*.

We know **supposed doesn't always work out**.

My first experience of a hater was in pre-school. It was over a Star Wars action figure. The dude hurt my arm, and I think I lost. The details are not clear, but it was probably one of my worst moments in my life even at that time. I couldn't believe I just fought with one of my schoolmates that was *supposed* to be nice to me and share.

I guess you can say that it was one of my first run-ins with a hater. Do you know what a hater is? In case you don't, I don't need the Merriam-Webster definition for this word. A hater is someone that doesn't like you, nor what you do. Period.

If it wasn't for the picture, I would have probably forgotten about this incident and wouldn't be telling you this story. As a kid, I believe there's one moment in our life that begins the timeline of when it all occurs. For me, it begun here.

There is always that one classmate that annoys, pesters or aggravates you in negative way (we're not talking about that brother or sister agitation). He or she calls you a name, makes fun of you, or physically hurts you. They might even try to exclude you. They can do all three, and some will do all three. You may not even know why, but they continue to pick on you for no reason or fault of your own. **That is bullying.**

In case you didn't realize it by now, I was one of those kids who were picked on. My differences of being black and fat stood out amongst the crowd. Throughout school, I learned my curly hair, dark skin, chubby cheeks, slow run and the clothes I wore were not like the others.

There is one memory that I still recall today, and still don't understand why they picked on me. I wore my brand new Nike Air Force Ones to school while I was in the 2nd grade. They were special. The shoes were blue, and the sole were bubble-gum colored.

The day was overcast in the Pacific Northwest. It was cool. No rain.

I was standing in line for my turn at tetherball. It all started with one kid pointing during lunch recess and saying,

> *"HEY EVERYONE! Check out Nathan's shoes! Look at the bottom, they're all different colors. HA-HA-HAH!"*

I'm thinking in my head that these shoes are "fresh", and I just picked them out from the Nike Outlet Store a couple of days ago. No one else has these. What was wrong with them?

The answer to that question, **nothing.**

Unfortunately, that was my introduction to my first group of haters. Not only were they hatin' on my new Nikes, they were also my very first nay-sayers. Nay-sayers are typically folks who are negative towards you and/or what you do. I got a 2-for-1 deal.

It was a double-whammy of a basic, *"You and your shoes suck!"*

I didn't understand why back then. I still somewhat don't understand why they had to attack my shoes of all things. The guy that started it all was named Jason, and I never liked him. We never became friends. Even though I tried to be cool with him, I really just didn't want him to pick on me again.

Back then, I didn't know my purpose to be at school was to learn. As I tell my son before he leaves for school every day, you go to school to learn and that's it. To make friends and playing on the playground is a bonus. Playing can be done anytime and anywhere, but your purpose needs be intentional. Focus on your purpose, and not on distractions.

We don't really think about it this way, but a common distraction would be any nay-sayer or hater of your purpose. Most wouldn't categorize them as this, but yes, they are a major distraction. They take you off task of that momentum you're building on, and create cracks in your foundation. Every attempt you make will be the ultimate failure, and will convince, persuade, or hint that your efforts aren't any good.

All that you have done becomes questioned. Your hard work isn't validated because they don't understand. That causes you pain and hurt, which shouldn't be the case. This is why you have to be careful your haters and nay-sayers don't fall under your supporting cast.

Please, please, please know that **family isn't excluded**. They don't get a "free pass" because they're blood. Guard yourself from all haters and nay-sayers. Negativity is negativity.

Here's a simple test. Do you have to ask them to support you? If you have to question their support, they may not be worthwhile to have around. Problem solved.

As you continue to live out your purpose, you may have to break down barriers, overcome unprecedented obstacles, or even trail blaze on your own path. Haters and nay-sayers are not welcome, nor invited.

Trail blazing is an individual effort.

TRAIL BLAZER

Have you ever heard of a trail blazer? And no, I'm not talking about the National Basketball Association professional team in Portland, Oregon. I'm talking about going off the trail, road, path, street, and making your own way.

The meaning of a trail blazer is that you create such an impactful force of doing your passion and purpose; people can't help but to follow in your footsteps.

Before we begin talking about making your own street, posting your name on Google maps, let me inform you that this is a lonely road **until your journey is celebrated**. Meaning, you will receive rewards and accolades throughout your journey without seeking them out. Parties will be thrown in your honor, and you honestly won't expect it because you're focused on not getting off track of your passion.

This will be a new navigational discovery. Some will not want to travel with you. Many obstacles and barriers will be in the way. You will have to stay determined for your vision to unfold.

Depending on your purpose and passion, some trails are in rainforests, deserts, oceans, and ice-lands. You won't know which terrain or obstacles that lay ahead of you, but that shouldn't stop you from starting.

Everything has a beginning. Some beginnings have easier starts than others, but all were forged with grit and determination. This is why we learn history, right?

We glorify our pioneers and inventors now, but the majority of them would never have imagined the glory and fame they have received if they would have listened to the nay-sayers and haters. If you really want to know what some of our geniuses did, complete the following:

Leonardo da Vinci painted the _ _ _ _   _ _ _ _.

Garret Morgan invented the _ _ _ _ _ _ _   _ _ _ _ _.

Steve Jobs started companies: _ _ _ _ _ & _ _ _ _ _.

This little activity is just the tip of the iceberg. If you follow up on those three individuals, you'll learn they faced enormous adversity. There wasn't any guarantee of rewards of fame or lots of cash. They **were all passionate** about their invention, because they believed it served a purpose.

Our purpose doesn't have to make the world news, but it also doesn't mean it couldn't go international. Do not set boundaries on your purpose. Only you can see your vision.

Let's apply this to our baker. Now that our pastry chef has their cookies down to a perfect science, we're closer to our dream. The customers are returning, and business is booming. Operations are an around-the-clock production. It's time to move out of the home kitchen, and get a bakery.

Great news, right? Yes, this is the day our baker has dreamed about from the very beginning. However, there is a problem. What type of bakery will the chef open?

Here are the options:

• Industrial space for bakery; sell to businesses and not walk-ins; no general public area.
• Industrial space for bakery; sell to local businesses and walk-ins; public can only walk-in and buy.
• Commercial space for bakery and restaurant; sell to all businesses and walk-ins; open to public and offer different menu items.

The above options are very basic, but all of them have a significant amount of details that need to be worked out.

Our pastry chef will have to do their own trail blazing to figure things out, because this isn't my dream. Everyone has their own trail blazing to do. **No one can bypass this step.** Another way to look at this is by leaving the distractions behind you.

Don't think of it as scary. Think of it as an exploration on the path to growth. You're in complete control, and you make the decisions. Nothing is going to happen that you don't want. Ultimately, you'll be creating everything that you want to happen.

To make this next step, one has to truly believe in their ability.

There cannot be any doubts.

BELIEVE

In this last chapter, I want to touch on something that is extremely important throughout the whole process of your journey. **Believe in yourself- always.** To believe is not just an isolated, one-time act. This is a true commitment to yourself and your goal. One of my favorite quotes is from Gandhi.

Mahatma Gandhi, a man who changed the world for many through his practice of non-violence.

"To believe in something, and not live it, is dishonest."

I was scared to be me, because I didn't believe in me. I didn't see value when I looked in the mirror. **I didn't believe I had a purpose.** I believed all the wrong things, which were all the mean stuff people said. It was never the uplifting, healthy, encouraging, reaffirming characteristics that everyone that believed in me saw. It wasn't until I finally got help and stood up for myself, I began to believe.

When we look at the simple definition of **Believe** from the dictionary, you'll see there should be no wavering. "To accept or regard (something) as true."

BELIEVE
: to accept or regard (something) as true
: to accept the truth of what is said by (someone)
: to have (a specified opinion)
: a person or animal that is killed in a sacrifice
Full Definition of **BELIEVE**
intransitive verb
1a : to have a firm religious faith
b : to accept something as true, genuine, or real <ideals we *believe* in><*believes* in ghosts>
2: to have a firm conviction as to the goodness, efficacy, or ability of something <*believe* in exercise>
3: to hold an opinion : THINK <I *BELIEVE* SO>

It's really simple, right?

To accept something is true doesn't include any trickery, magic, money, education, or status. You either believe or you don't. There's no chemistry, physics, or other science to figure it out. You either believe or you don't.

So now, let's apply this simple principal to you. Look at the palm of your hands. Hold them side by side. Begin to clinch them slowly. As you do this, say one or all of the following:

For ex.: ***I am smart; I can be** a scientist; **I believe** I am intelligent; **I will** be one of the world's best physicists.*

Now it's your turn and fill-in the blanks:

I am _____!

I can _____!

I believe I am _____!

I will _____!

Begin to clinch them slowly, and say it.

Now, say it with conviction. Believe in your heart that it's true!

For years as a child, teenager, and as an adult, I couldn't say one good thing about myself. For example, I played soccer all my life, and I was at my best when I played goalkeeper. I was pretty decent at it, but I didn't know how good I was until my sophomore year in high school.

My team was nationally ranked. They had won 3 state titles in a row. I made the varsity traveling roster, but I was still on the junior varsity squad. However, the team was on our 4th trip up to the state semi-finals and finals to earn the 4th state title in a row.

Even though I didn't play during the playoffs, my coach always told me to be ready. I'm looking at him thinking he was crazy. I was the 3rd string goalkeeper. The starter was awesome. His backup was great, and I was cool with just watching. My season just ended with junior varsity. I was ok with enjoying the ride to have fun.

During practice one day, my coach told me the starter goalkeeper had a family emergency. He didn't know if he was going to play in the game, but I had to be ready just in case. When he told me that, we weren't at our normal practice field at Mountain View High School in Vancouver, WA. We were practicing in a stadium Downtown Portland, OR where the Major League Soccer Portland Timbers play.

I looked up at all the stands, and it was so surreal. I started playing soccer in the 1st grade because I was excited that I got to wear a jersey to school from time to time. I never once believed I would have the opportunity to play on a professional soccer field. And here I was, playing with the best players in the state **still in disbelief** that I belonged there.

Believing is a constant thought to fuel your passion. Think of it as a car. Believing is the equivalent to gasoline. Cars are the equivalent to your dream. Your tank is either full, empty, or somewhere in between.

Have you noticed the streets and highways are filled with moving cars? Without fuel, we cannot move. It is the GO we need to live our purpose.

To not believe are those abandoned cars on side of the highway. They're always vacant. Some look worn down. There are even some that look brand new. Nonetheless, they're still not moving and could be other reasons than fuel. Yet again, their ability to go has been disabled.

Your belief in your abilities is the ground of your foundation. Believing will ensure your building blocks remain solid and strong. Everything and anything you do will succeed because you're building on your belief system. It cannot fall or fail unless you stop believing. Once that moment occurs, every bonding mechanism that is in place will undo. Therefore, always believe.

No matter if you believe a little or a lot, believe. You may not know how it may look, it's ok. That's when you trail blaze.

Always believe.

Don't let the work of the bare land scare you from building your palace. Even the baker needed to start somewhere. No one else may support you, it's ok. You don't need a big supporting cast. If you made it this far, continue to believe and don't look back.

BELIEVE IN:

YOU

HOPE

DREAMS

MENTORS

HARD WORK

EDUCATION

EXERCISE

HEALTH

CONCLUSION: DON'T LOOK BACK

By now, you have already began looking back to think of what you could have, would have, or should have done (and no, you're not too young for this). Well, now is the time to use those regrets as your motivation. Make those regrets work for your benefit.

As the old saying goes, "hindsight is 20/20."

You can always look back and critique yourself on your past events, but make sure you have takeaways. A **takeaway** is an actionable step. This can be to fix what you did or didn't like. My advice is to have at least two takeaways: one positive and one negative. And yes, I believe you can have more, but at least have those two so you can begin making those adjustments to what you want.

I admit - I have thought about what would have happened if I hadn't joined the Marine Corps, or if I had not attended a four year university. Instead of the United States Marine Corps and my educational experience at a 4-year university, everything would be different.

If I took the education path first, I would have missed experiencing different cultures (i.e. – Hawaii, Japan, and military lifestyle). I would have not had my same professors in college who have molded my current life. And the main issue, I would have not found the need to start my own nonprofit if I believed college was easy.

Every person that is vitally important to my life now, our paths wouldn't have crossed the same intersections.

Even though I would love to say that I could have accomplished my dreams without some of those people and bad times, I cannot deny that I met a lot of great (and even famous) people, seen amazing once-in-a-lifetime events, and accomplished personal milestones. Focusing on the bad is easy and depressing, but reminiscing on the good brings smiles, laughter, and more happiness to my life.

There's way more events that make me proud to have lived my life.

In all honesty, I wouldn't change a thing if I had to do it again. Would I be grimacing and grinding my teeth while I'll have to make these bad decisions again? OH YEAH! It would be really painful to watch me re-live bad relationships, horrible mistakes, and dumb decisions over again. However, I would know that determines my future.

As the saying goes, "*You don't know what you don't know.*" In which goes into the next saying, "*What doesn't kill you, makes you stronger.*"

Here's a really simple saying that you probably already know. "*You're not perfect.*" So stop trying to make everything perfect. Making adjustments will be a never-ending battle.

If you don't accept that mistakes are part of maturity and personal growth, you will live a self-inflicted hard life. Perfection doesn't apply to humans. We're not infallible nor perfect. Therefore, stop trying to be perfect or waiting for a perfect opportunity.

To be you is perfect. You may not do everything perfect, but no one does. You are perfect in your own way. There's no comparison to you. You and your purpose is unique.

No more being scared.

Be you!

Dream Big!

I've learned…

1. _____

2. _____

3. _____

My Steps

☐ _____

☐ _____

☐ _____

☐ _____

☐ _____

☐ _____

☐ _____

BIBLIOGRAPHY

Academy of Achievement. *Frederick W. Smith Biography*. 2 May 2014. http://www.achievement.org/autodoc/page/smi0bio-1. 26 October 2014.

Burfoot, Amby. "Ultimate 100-Meter Time: 9.27 Seconds?" *Runner's World & Running Times* 14 June 2014: Newswire. http://www.runnersworld.com/elite-runners/ultimate-100-meter-time-927-seconds.

FedEx. *History of FedEx Operating Companies*. 14 August 2013. http://about.van.fedex.com/fedex-opco-history. 26 October 2014.

Matt3756. *Coin Pusher Tutorial + Tips*. 26 May 2012. https://www.youtube.com/watch?v=HLwIOk-0jpc. 26 October 2014.

Merriam-Webster, Incorporated. *Merriam-Webster Dictionary: Believe*. 2014. http://www.merriam-webster.com/dictionary/believe. 26 October 2014.

—. *Merriam-Webster Dictionary: Eminence*. 2014. http://www.merriam-webster.com/dictionary/eminence?show=0&t=1411304838. 26 October 2014.

—. *Merriam-Webster Dictionary: Outcome*. 2014. http://www.merriam-webster.com/dictionary/outcome?show=0&t=1411306710. 26 October 2014.

—. *Merriam-Webster Dictionary: Sacrifice*. 2014. http://www.merriam-webster.com/dictionary/sacrifice. 26 October 2014.

—. *Merriam-Webster Dictionary: Succeed*. 2014. http://www.merriam-webster.com/dictionary/succeed?show=0&t=1411303141. 26 October 2014.

—. *Merriam-Webster Dictionary: Success*. 2014. http://www.merriam-webster.com/dictionary/success. 26 October 2014.

Motor Trend. "Maxximus G-Force: The Fastest Car in the World?" *Motor Trend* February 2009. http://www.motortrend.com/features/auto_news/2009/112_0902_maxximus_g_force/.

Nike, Inc. *Executives: Nike, Inc.* 2014. http://about.nike.com/pages/executives. 26 October 2014.

The Travel Almanac. *The Fastest Fish in the World*. 29 August 2014. http://www.thetravelalmanac.com/lists/fish-speed.htm. 26 October 2014.

—. *The World's Fastest Birds*. 29 August 2014. http://www.thetravelalmanac.com/lists/birds-speed.htm. 26 October 2014.

—. *The World's Fastest Mammals*. 29 August 2014. http://www.thetravelalmanac.com/lists/mammals-speed.htm. 26 October 2014.

Wayne, Leslie. "For $305 Million, Nike Buys Converse." *The New York Times* 10 July 2003: Archive. http://www.nytimes.com/2003/07/10/business/10NIKE.html

Trail Blazer Trivia

Mona Lisa

Traffic Light

Apple & Pixar

Printed in the United States
By Bookmasters